FORCES AND MOVEMENT (PUSH, PULL, FAST, SLOW AND MORE) 2ND GRADE SCIENCE WORKBOOK CHILDREN'S PHYSICS BOOKS EDITION

SPEEDY
PUBLISHING

Speedy Publishing LLC
40 E. Main St. #1156
Newark, DE 19711
www.speedypublishing.com

Physics is a branch of science that studies matter and its motion as well as how it interacts with energy and forces.

In physics,
force is
a push or
pull on an
object.

A force can cause an object to accelerate, slow down, remain in place, or change shape.

Pushing moves something in the direction of the push.

The harder
the push,
the further
the item
goes.

Pulling something has a similar action. The harder you pull, the faster something moves along.

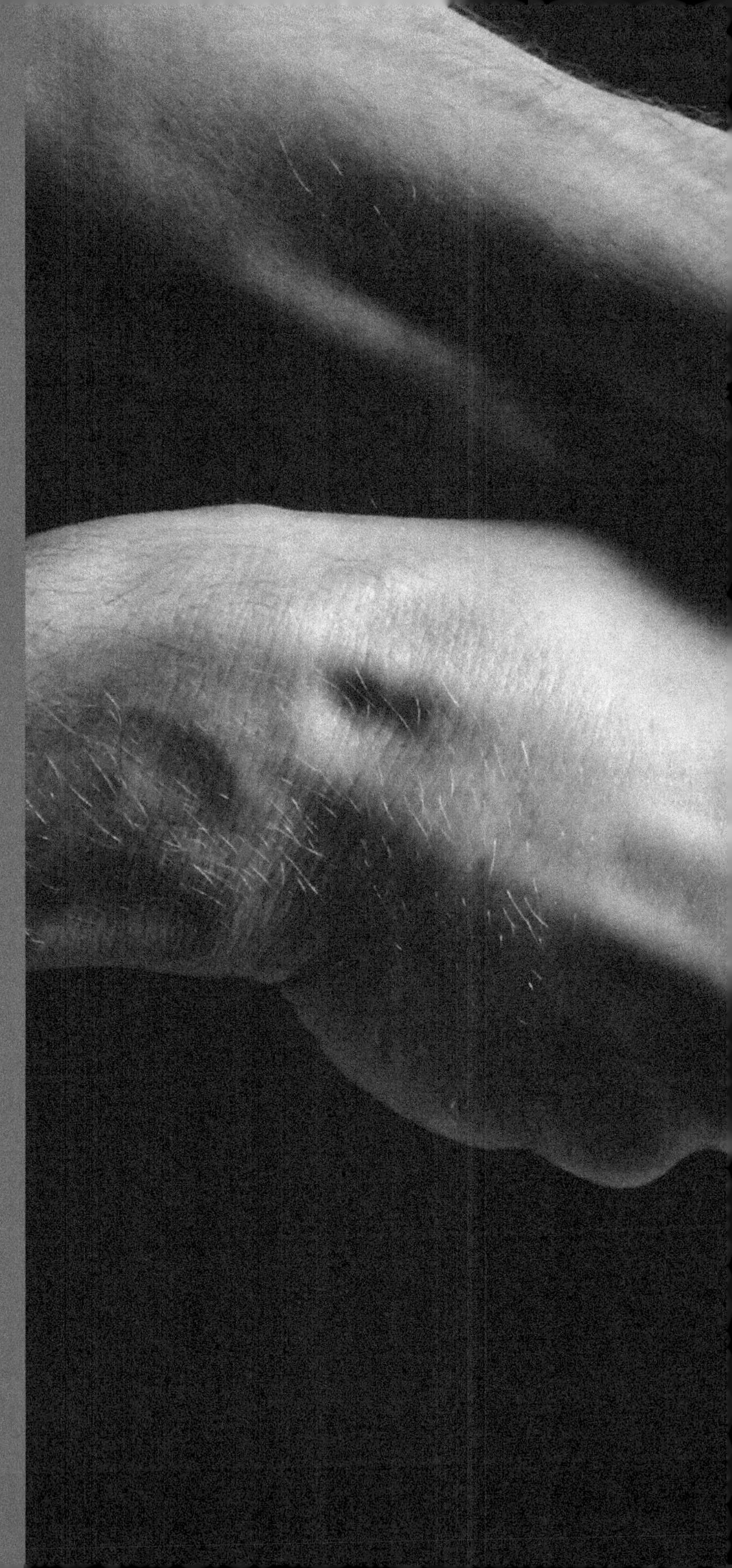
A force
has both
magnitude
and
direction,
making it
a vector
quantity.

Springs and elastic are also types of force. Push against them and they resist.

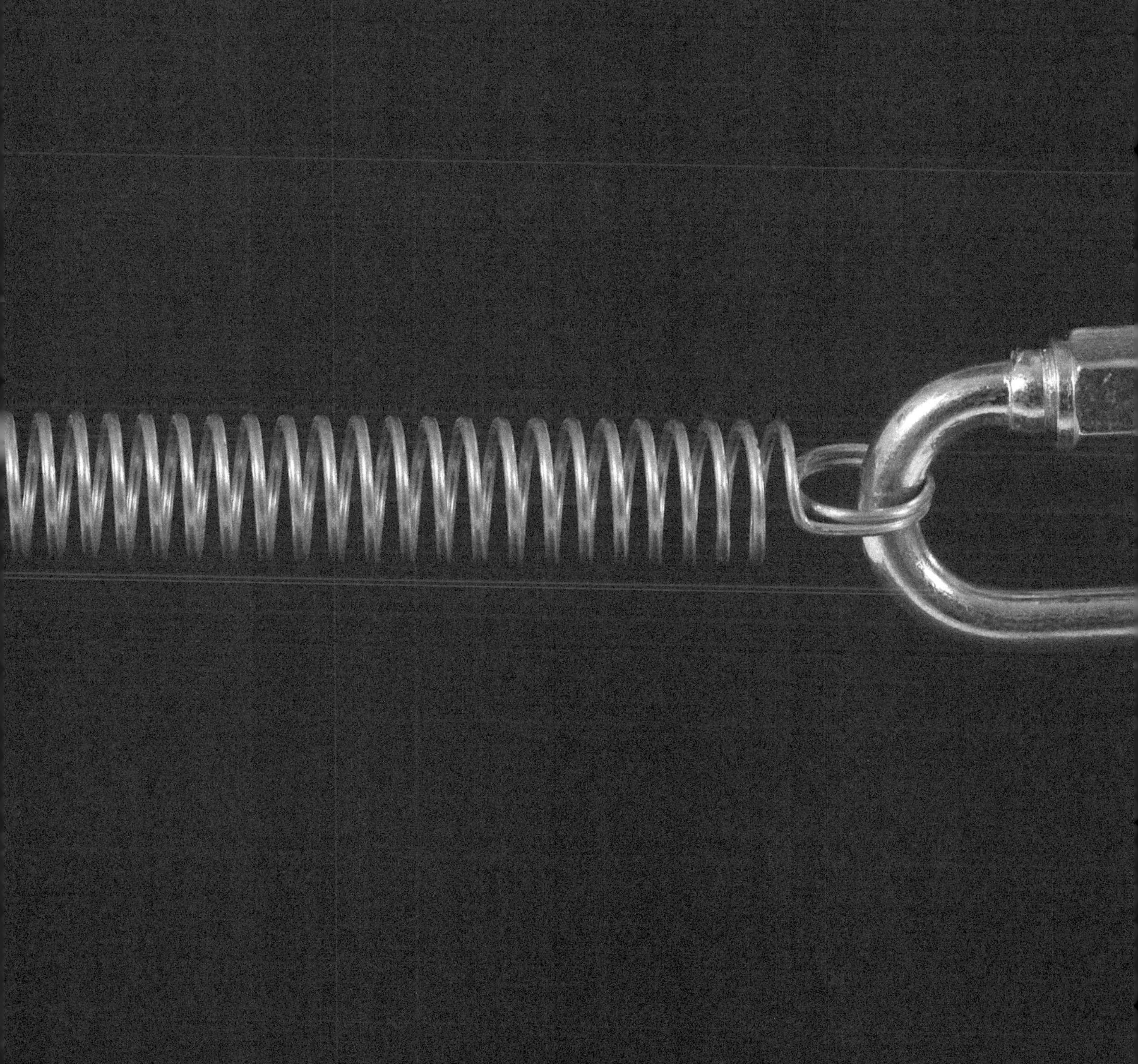

Forces are measured in units called newtons, named after English scientist Sir Isaac Newton.

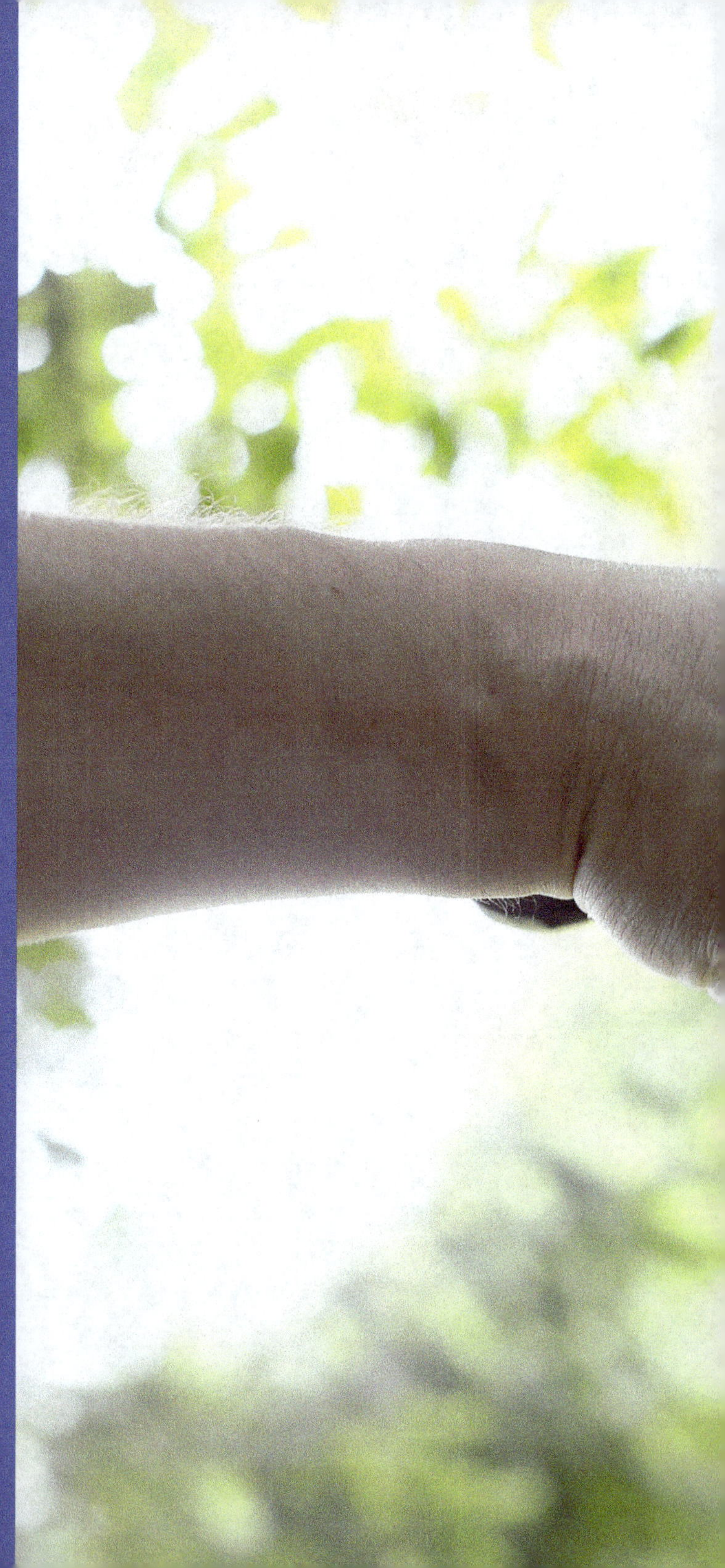

Motion
is the
changing
of position
or location.

But motion requires a force to cause that change.

A scientist named Isaac Newton came up with three Laws of Motion to describe how things move.

The first law says that any object in motion will continue to move in the same direction and speed unless forces act on it.

The second law states that the greater the mass of an object, the more force it will take to accelerate the object.

The third law states that for every action, there is an equal and opposite reaction.

FINISH

When
a force
in one
direction
changes
the speed
of an
object,
this is
known as
acceleration.

Speed
means
things
moving
fast or
slow.

Speed is defined as the distance an object travels in a certain amount of time.

Velocity is the speed of an object moving in a particular direction.

Visit

www.BabyProfessorBooks.com

to download Free Baby Professor eBooks
and view our catalog of new and exciting
Children's Books